curious NATURE

ANIMALS

QUESTIONS & ANSWERS

NANCY DICKMANN

W

FRANKLIN WATTS

LONDON • SYDNEY

First published in Great Britain in 2017 by
The Watts Publishing Group

Copyright © 2017 Brown Bear Books Ltd

For Brown Bear Books Ltd:
Text and Editor: Nancy Dickmann
Editorial Director: Lindsey Lowe
Children's Publisher: Anne O'Daly
Design Manager: Keith Davis
Designer and Illustrator: Supriya Sahai
Picture Manager: Sophie Mortimer

Concept development: Square and Circus/Brown Bear
Books Ltd

ISBN: 978 1 4451 5672 9

Printed in Malaysia

Franklin Watts
An imprint of
Hachette Children's Group
Part of the Watts Publishing Group
Carmelite House
50 Victoria Embankment
London EC4Y 0DZ

An Hachette UK company
www.hachette.co.uk
www.franklinwatts.co.uk

Websites
The website addresses (URLs) included in this book
were valid at the time of going to press. However,
it is possible that contents or addresses may change
following the publication of this book. No responsibility
for any such changes can be accepted by either the
author or the publisher.

CONTENTS

WHAT ARE ANIMALS?

Animals are living creatures. They come in all shapes and sizes, from tiny ants to enormous elephants. They live in forests, oceans, deserts and grasslands. Some live in our homes or on our bodies! Animals can be scaly, slimy, furry or feathery. Some animals can fly, while others run or swim.

All animals have some things in common. They move and grow. They take in food and get rid of waste. Their bodies use food and oxygen to produce energy. They respond to the world around them. They produce babies who grow up to look like them.

ANIMAL SURVIVORS

Animals can live almost anywhere. Emperor penguins live in Antarctica. It is cold and snowy all year round. Other animals live in very hot places. Animals even live in dry deserts. They have clever ways of finding water.

CORAL

Corals grow in shallow oceans. They are attached to the sea floor. Corals look like plants. But they are actually made up of thousands of tiny animals. These tiny animals have tentacles that sweep food into their mouths.

WHAT IS A MAMMAL?

A mammal is a type of animal. Mammals can be big or small. Elephants are mammals and so are mice. Humans are mammals, too!

Mammals live on land or in the ocean. They all have hair or fur. Their babies are born alive, instead of hatching from an egg. A mammal mother produces milk to feed her babies.

LIFE IN A POUCH

Some mammal mothers have a pouch on their belly. Their babies are tiny when they are born. They stay in the pouch and drink milk. When they are big enough, they come out of the pouch.

A wallaby carries its baby in a pouch.

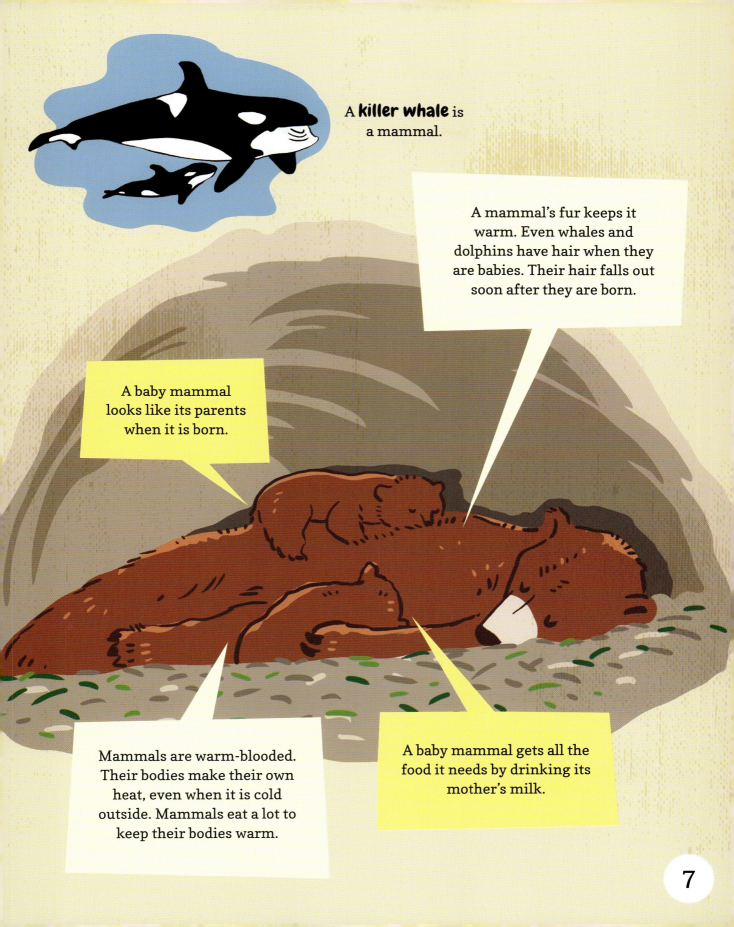

A **killer whale** is a mammal.

A mammal's fur keeps it warm. Even whales and dolphins have hair when they are babies. Their hair falls out soon after they are born.

A baby mammal looks like its parents when it is born.

Mammals are warm-blooded. Their bodies make their own heat, even when it is cold outside. Mammals eat a lot to keep their bodies warm.

A baby mammal gets all the food it needs by drinking its mother's milk.

WHY DO LIZARDS LIE IN THE SUN?

Lizards are a type of reptile. Reptiles are not warm-blooded, like mammals are. They are cold-blooded. Their bodies do not make their own heat. A lizard's body gets cold when it is cold outside. It cannot move very well when it is cold. It lies in the sun, in a warm place. The sun heats up the lizard's body. Then it can move more easily.

A crocodile has sharp teeth for catching animals to eat.

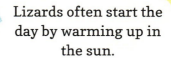

Lizards often start the day by warming up in the sun.

Reptiles have dry, scaly skin. It helps them to survive in dry places.

A lizard uses its sharp claws to climb, run and catch food.

Lizards have four legs for running and walking. Some reptiles, such as snakes, have no legs.

SCALES AND SHELLS

Lizards, crocodiles, snakes and alligators are all reptiles. Turtles and tortoises are reptiles, too. They have hard shells that protect their bodies.

All reptiles have tails. Some use their tails for swimming or holding on to branches. Some lizards have a tail that breaks off if another animal grabs it. Then the lizard can escape.

9

WHICH ANIMAL HAS THE MOST LEGS?

Legs are very useful. They help animals to stand, walk and run. You have two legs, and so do birds. Dogs and cats have four legs. But some animals have even more.

The record for the most legs belongs to a type of millipede. It can have up to 750 legs! Even with so many legs, it doesn't move very fast. This is because its legs are very short.

Birds use their feet to hold on to branches.

ONE FOOT?

Many animals have no legs at all. Snails and slugs have just a single foot! Their bodies are like a stomach and foot joined together.

An **ant** is a type of insect. All insects have six legs.

Spiders look like insects, but they are different. They have eight legs. Scorpions and ticks are related to spiders. They have eight legs, too.

A **centipede's** name means '100 feet'. But no one has ever found a centipede with exactly 100 legs! Some have just 28, and others have more than 300.

A **millipede's** name means '1,000 feet'. They usually have hundreds of legs.

HOW DO FISH BREATHE UNDERWATER?

All animals need oxygen. Oxygen is a gas that is found in the air. It helps animals produce the energy they need. Getting oxygen is easy for animals that live on land. All they have to do is breathe!

Fish live underwater, so they get oxygen in a different way. They have special body parts called gills. Their gills let oxygen in the water move into the fish's blood.

Mudskippers are fish that can go on land. They get oxygen through their skin.

12

Sharks are a kind of fish. They have two sets of **gills**. The gills are just behind their mouth.

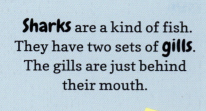

BREATHING AIR

Mammals like dolphins and whales live underwater, too. They do not have gills. Instead, they come to the surface to breathe. They can hold their breath for a long time.

INSIDE A SHARK'S HEAD

Water comes in through the shark's mouth.

The gills are full of tiny blood vessels. Water flows past the gills. Oxygen moves from the water into the blood. Then the water flows out of the gills.

13

CAN ANIMALS CHANGE COLOUR?

Animals come in many different colours. Some animals are just one colour. Others have lots of colours. A few animals can change colour! Some do this to blend in with the background. This makes it harder for predators to see them.

Some animals change colour to frighten other animals away. Some change colour when they are scared or to attract a mate.

An Arctic fox's fur turns white in winter to blend in with the snow.

CHANGING SHAPE

The harmless mimic octopus can change its colour and its shape! It can make itself look like a lion fish or sea snake. These animals are poisonous. Other animals are afraid to attack them.

A cuttlefish can change colour in less than a second.

The skin is made up of millions of tiny cells. Each one has a job.

The brain sends signals to the skin when a cuttlefish wants to change colour.

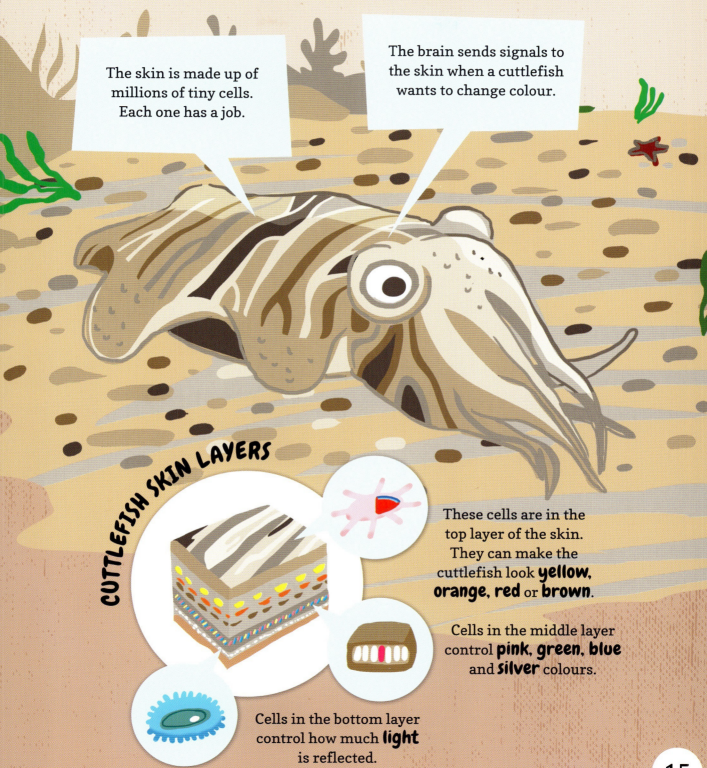

CUTTLEFISH SKIN LAYERS

These cells are in the top layer of the skin. They can make the cuttlefish look **yellow, orange, red** or **brown**.

Cells in the middle layer control **pink, green, blue** and **silver** colours.

Cells in the bottom layer control how much **light** is reflected.

WHY DO ZEBRAS HAVE STRIPES?

Scientists aren't sure why zebras have stripes. One idea is that the stripes are a kind of camouflage. Animals use camouflage to blend in and hide.

Zebras often travel in big groups. When a lion sees a crowd of black and white stripes, it is hard to pick out one animal to chase. When a group of zebras is on the move, their stripes can make it look like the zebras are going in a different direction.

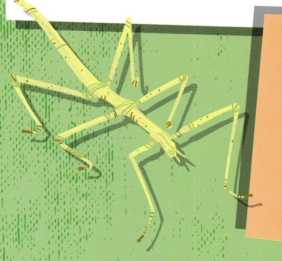

SPOT THE INSECT

Some animals have a different kind of camouflage. Their bodies look like something else. For example, a walking-stick insect looks like a twig. That helps it to hide.

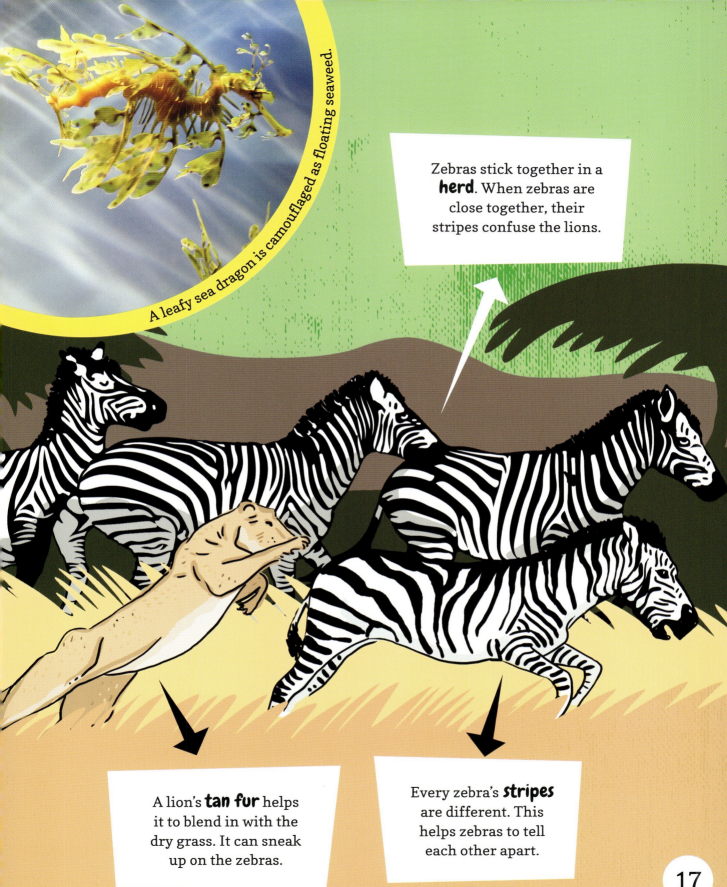

A leafy sea dragon is camouflaged as floating seaweed.

Zebras stick together in a **herd**. When zebras are close together, their stripes confuse the lions.

A lion's **tan fur** helps it to blend in with the dry grass. It can sneak up on the zebras.

Every zebra's **stripes** are different. This helps zebras to tell each other apart.

CAN ANIMALS USE TOOLS?

Humans use tools to help to do jobs. Our tools range from hammers to high-tech robots. Some animals use tools too! The tools help them to reach food, keep dry or stay safe. Most animals use objects that they find. A few animals can make their own tools.

UMBRELLAS

Orangutans sometimes use leaves as tools. They choose big leaves to use as umbrellas when it rains. They also use leaves to shelter from the hot sun.

Bottlenose dolphins use sponges as tools. The sponges protect their noses as they dig for fish in the sand.

Elephants use branches to swat flies.

Some **crows** hold sticks in their beaks. They use them to pry insects out of wood.

A **sea otter** floats on its back. It holds a stone on its chest. It bangs a mussel against the stone to open the shell for food.

One kind of **octopus** collects coconut shells. It uses them to build shelters.

A **chimpanzee** uses a big stick to dig a hole in a termite mound. Then it uses a smaller stick to fish out termites to eat.

WHICH ANIMAL IS THE FASTEST?

The cheetah is the fastest runner of all. It can reach speeds of 113 kilometres per hour! The cheetah uses its speed to chase other animals. It hunts gazelles, antelopes and warthogs. Cheetahs' bodies are built for speed. They have special features that help the animal to move faster.

Tiger beetles are the fastest insects, running at 9 kilometres per hour.

A cheetah's **long tail** helps with steering and balance.

BUILT FOR SPEED

A big, **powerful heart** keeps blood pumping to the muscles.

The **long spine** is very flexible. It lets the cheetah take longer strides.

Large lungs take in lots of air.

Cheetahs don't weigh very much. Their bodies are **slim,** with small heads and long legs.

Blunt claws and rough pads help the paws to grip the ground.

WHY DO SALMON SWIM UPSTREAM?

Salmon are born in flowing freshwater rivers and streams. Young adult salmon migrate to live in the sea. There, they feed and grow large. After a few years, they return to the same place they were born. They battle their way upstream to mate and lay their eggs. Swimming against the flow of the water is tiring. Only the strongest fish make it back.

Adult salmon dig nests in gravel. They lay **eggs** in the nests.

In spring, the eggs hatch under the gravel. The **young fish** have yolk sacs they use for food.

After a few weeks the small fish leave the nest. They are now called **fry**. They feed on tiny organisms in the water.

ANADROMOUS LIFE CYCLE

'Anadromous' means salmon start their lives in fresh water. They migrate to the sea to grow and feed. The adult salmon return to lay eggs in fresh water.

When the adult salmon return, they are known as **kelts**. They look thin and tired. Some make it back to the sea, but most will die.

The salmon grow big in the sea. Large **adult salmon** head for home to lay their own eggs.

The parr change into **smolts**, just before the salmon head out to sea. Smolts are covered in silvery scales.

Salmon sometimes have to jump when they swim upstream.

Salmon over one year old are known as **parr**. They are still small. They still live in fresh water.

WHAT IS THE BIGGEST ANIMAL?

If you guessed elephant, think again. A dinosaur? That's not right either. The biggest animal that ever existed is still alive today. It is the mighty blue whale. This gentle giant swims through the world's oceans. It can be 30 metres long.

The blue whale eats tiny sea creatures called krill. The whale opens its giant mouth to gulp water. Then it lets the water out. Fringed plates called baleen trap the krill inside.

The krill that the blue whale eats are about as long as your finger.

SUPER-SMALL

Not all mammals are big. The Etruscan shrew is about 5 centimetres long. It weighs less than a penny. The bumblebee bat is the size of a large bumbleebee. It is only 3 centimetres long!

Blue whales make noises that are louder than **a jet engine!**

Blue whales weigh up to 181 tonnes. That's the same as **24 elephants.**

A blue whale's heart can weigh 680 kilograms. That's the size of **a cow.**

A blue whale can be 30 metres long. That's longer than **three buses.**

A blue whale can eat 3.6 tonnes of krill in one day. That's like eating **a whole hippo!**

HOW DO CATERPILLARS TURN INTO BUTTERFLIES?

Bright, colourful butterflies start life as eggs. Their bodies change shape completely as they grow. This is called metamorphosis.

Other animals go through metamorphosis, too. Frog spawn hatch into tadpoles. They have tails but no legs. Then the tadpoles lose their tails and grow legs, turning into frogs.

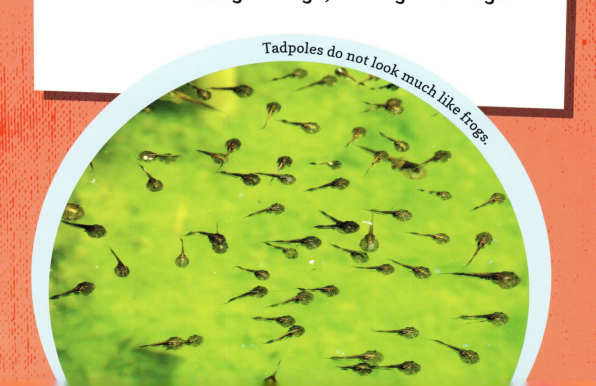

Tadpoles do not look much like frogs.

SILK

Moth caterpillars make cases called cocoons. The cocoon made by the silk moth caterpillar is very special. It is made of thin fibres that the caterpillar produces. These fibres can be woven into soft silk cloth.

The caterpillar turns itself into a **chrysalis**. This is a hard case that hangs in a safe place. Inside, the caterpillar changes into a butterfly.

BUTTERFLY LIFE CYCLE

The **caterpillar** hatches from the egg. It eats leaves and grows. When its outer skin gets too tight, it splits open. There is a new, bigger skin underneath.

An adult butterfly lays **eggs** on a leaf. Inside each egg, a tiny caterpillar takes shape.

The chrysalis splits open. A **butterfly** comes out. It finds a mate and the cycle begins again.

MAKE A BUG HOTEL

Your garden or park has lots of creepy-crawlies like insects, spiders, worms and snails. Why not make a home for them? Build a fantastic bug hotel out of recycled materials.

WHAT YOU NEED

* old bricks or large stones
* planks of wood
* straw
* twigs
* pine cones
* moss
* dry leaves
* bark
* bamboo sticks

1 Choose a place for your bug hotel. It should be against a wall or fence in a shady spot.

2 Put some bricks on the ground. Lay a plank across the top.

3 Add more bricks and planks until you have a few levels.

4 Each level can have a different kind of home. Tie a bundle of twigs together or stick them in a cardboard tube.

Be creative with your bug hotel!

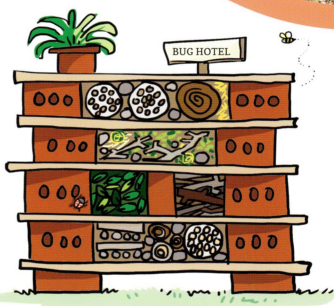

BUG HOTEL

5 Make a nest of dry leaves, moss and bark on another level.

WATCH YOUR BUG HOTEL

As the weeks pass, your bug hotel should fill up. Check it every few days, but try not to disturb the animals. Keep a list of the different kinds of animals you see.

6 Add pine cones and straw. Add small tubes such as reeds or bamboo sticks for bees.

GLOSSARY

blood vessel tube inside the body that blood flows through

camouflage way of hiding something by using colours and patterns

cell one of the tiny building blocks that make up all life

desert place that gets very little rain

energy ability to do work

gills parts of a fish's body that help it to get oxygen from the water

grassland large area of land covered by grass

hatch to be born from an egg

herd large group of animals, such as zebras or antelope, that travel and feed together

insect small animal with six legs. Bees, ants, beetles and butterflies are all insects.

mammal type of animal that has hair or fur and makes milk to feed its babies

metamorphosis process in which an animal changes shape as it grows

nutrient substance that a living thing needs in order to survive and grow

oxygen gas in the air that animals need

predator animal that hunts other animals to eat

reptile type of cold-blooded animal with dry, scaly skin. Crocodiles, turtles and snakes are reptiles.

spine another name for the backbone. It is made up of many smaller bones.

tentacle long, thin part on the head or near the mouth of some animals. Tentacles can be used for feeling or grabbing.

FURTHER RESOURCES

BOOKS

Animals (Find Out!),
Dorling Kindersley (DK, 2016)

Awesome Animals: Facts, Stats and Quizzes
(Stat Attack!), Tracey Turner (Franklin Watts, 2015)

Over 1000 Fantastic Animal Facts,
(Miles Kelly, 2011)

Super Nature: The 100 Biggest Fastest,
Deadliest Creatures on the Planet, (DK, 2012)

Why Do Zebras Have Stripes?:
Questions and Answers About Animals,
Thomas Canavan (Franklin Watts, 2015)

WEBSITES

discoverykids.com/category/animals
The Discovery Channel's children's web pages contain
games, videos, facts and activities about animals.

www.bbc.co.uk/cbbc/topics/animals
Videos, photos, facts and quizzes about animals from
CBBC, with links to BBC nature programmes.

www.ngkids.co.uk/animals
National Geographic Kids web pages with facts and
quizzes about all kinds of different animals.

INDEX